IN MY BACKYARD

mice

by Kate Riggs

CREATIVE EDUCATION • CREATIVE PAPERBACKS

Published by Creative Education and Creative Paperbacks
P.O. Box 227, Mankato, Minnesota 56002
Creative Education and Creative Paperbacks are imprints of
The Creative Company
www.thecreativecompany.us

Design and production by Chelsey Luther
Art direction by Rita Marshall
Printed in China

Photographs by Alamy (LISA MOORE, National Geographic
Image Collection, Florian Schulz), Matt Binstead (Matt
Binstead/British Wildlife Centre), Corbis (Mike Kemp/Tetra
Images), Dreamstime (Alptraum, Pavel Chernobrivets, Icefront,
Maxim Kulko, Ljupco Smokovski, Yurakp, Rudmer Zwerver),
iStockphoto (GlobalP), Science Source (Jean-Louis Klein &
Marie-Luce Hubert), Shutterstock (CreativeNature R.Zwerver,
Eric Isselee, Szasz-Fabian Jozsef, kontur-vid, rayjunk, schankz)

Library of Congress Cataloging-in-Publication Data
Riggs, Kate.
Mice / by Kate Riggs.
p. cm. — (In my backyard)
Includes bibliographical references and index.
Summary: A high-interest introduction to the life cycle of
mice, including how pinkies develop, their plant-based diet,
threats from predators, and the woodsy habitats of these
backyard animals.

ISBN 978-1-60818-699-0 (hardcover)
ISBN 978-1-62832-295-8 (pbk)
ISBN 978-1-56660-735-3 (eBook)
1. Mice—Juvenile literature.

QL737.R6 R534 2016
599.35—dc23   2015034574

CCSS: RI.1.1, 2, 3, 4, 5, 6, 7; RI.2.1, 2, 4, 5, 6, 7, 10; RF.1.1, 3, 4;
RF.2.3, 4

First Edition HC 9 8 7 6 5 4 3 2 1
First Edition PBK 9 8 7 6 5 4 3 2 1

Contents

Bits of paper are on the floor. Chewed-up wires stick out of the wall. You see a tail disappear into a small hole. A mouse is making a nest in your house!

Mice can squeeze through openings as small as a dime.

Baby mice are pink at first. They do not have fur. They are called pinkies. Four to 12 pinkies are born in a litter. Baby mice are also called pups. Pups grow to become adults in six to eight weeks.

field mouse

The house mouse is a common species that is found near people. You may see deer mice where you live, too. Deer mice have larger eyes than house mice. They also have white bellies and white feet.

house mouse

Deer mice (right) are so named because their fur looks like a deer's.

Mice are active at night. They stay quiet most of the day. Some mice live in burrows. Mice like to live near places where they can find food.

When they are not eating, mice usually sleep more than 12 hours a day.

Mice eat plant parts like seeds, grains, and fruits. Only cartoon mice eat cheese! Sometimes mice will eat meat or other foods, too.

Mice use their two front paws to hold on to food when they eat.

Mice eat 15 to 20 times a day! They guard their food and nest sites. They do not want other mice to steal anything. Mice that live near a lot of food do not fight over it.

Wood mice (left) dig their own burrow systems to live in and store food.

M ice that live in fields and woods have many preda-tors. Birds, cats, foxes, and snakes hunt for mice.

Mice avoid predators by using their great senses of hearing and smelling.

A mouse in the house can make a mess! Outside, it is free to run, jump, and climb anywhere. Look for mice near piles of leaves and under bushes. You might scare them!

A scared mouse might stop moving or hide in the closest shelter.

Activity: Nesting Behavior

Female mice build nests. They chew up whatever they can find to make a soft place for their babies. What if you were a mouse? What would you use to make a nest?

Materials you need: old newspapers and magazines, blankets, towels, clothing items; pencil and notebook

The Best Nest

1. With an adult's permission, tear up paper from newspapers and magazines. Pile it up in a corner or some other place where no one will trip over it. Try lying down on the pile. Is it comfortable? Is it noisy? Use a notebook to record what you find out.

2. What if you used a bunch of towels or jackets instead? Add a blanket or two to the pile. Write down what your nest feels like. Is it soft and lumpy?

3. Draw a picture of yourself in your nest. Then be sure to put everything away. You aren't a messy mouse!

Think about why a mother mouse would want to build a nest. Do you like to sleep in a soft, warm place?

 Glossary

burrows: holes or tunnels dug in the ground

litter: a group of animal babies born at the same time; mice can have up to 10 litters a year

predators: animals that hunt other animals for food

species: groups of living things that are closely related

Read More

Markle, Sandra. *Outside and Inside Rats and Mice.*
New York: Atheneum, 2001.

Schuetz, Kari. *Mice.*
Minneapolis: Bellwether Media, 2014.

Websites

National Geographic Kids: The Big Gulp
http://kids.nationalgeographic.com/games/quick-play
/the-big-gulp/
Help a mouse through a maze, and watch a Zooville video
about house mice!

National Wildlife Federation: Leaf Mice
http://www.nwf.org/kids/family-fun/crafts/leaf-mice.aspx
Follow the directions to make mice out of leaves.

Note: Every effort has been made to ensure that the websites listed above are suitable for
children, that they have educational value, and that they contain no inappropriate mate-
rial. However, because of the nature of the Internet, it is impossible to guarantee that these
sites will remain active indefinitely or that their contents will not be altered.

Index